TOLSTOY IN LOVE

First published in 2009 by
Dedalus Press
13 Moyclare Road
Baldoyle
Dublin 13
Ireland

www.dedaluspress.com

Copyright © Ray Givans, 2009

ISBN 978 1 906614 08 9

All rights reserved.
No part of this publication may be reproduced in any form or by
any means without the prior permission of the publisher.

Dedalus Press titles are represented in North America
by Syracuse University Press, Inc., 621 Skytop Road,
Suite 110, Syracuse, New York 13244, and in the UK by
Central Books, 99 Wallis Road, London E9 5LN

Cover image © Auke Holwerda/iStockPhoto.com

Dedalus Press receives financial
assistance from The Arts Council

Tolstoy in Love

Ray Givans

DEDALUS PRESS
DUBLIN, IRELAND

ACKNOWLEDGEMENTS

To the editors of the following publications in which a number of these poems originally appeared:

Anglican Theological Review, Envoi, Equinox, Fire, Iota, Orbis, Other Poetry, Pennine Platform, Penumbra, Poetry Ireland Review, Poetry Scotland, Rustic Rub, The SHOp and *Third Way.*

A number of poems were collected in the following anthologies:

Artwords (2000); *Before Winter* (Grendon House, Isle of Lewis, 2000); *Bluechrome Poetry Competition Winners' Anthology, 2006; Earth Works*—in collaboration with artist Tony Martin (Subway, Bristol, 2003); *Going Home* (Lapwing Publications, 2004); *Miracle and Clockwork* (anthology selection from ten years of Other Poetry magazine, 2006); *No Surrender Castlecaulfield* (Lapwing Publications, 1993).

'Anna Akhmatova' was awarded first prize in The Studio Open Poetry Competition, Australia.

Contents

ONE
Tolstoy in Love

Anna Akhmatova / 9
Tolstoy in Love / 10
Sonya Tolstoy / 11
The Jealousy of Sonya Tolstoy / 13
Sonya Tolstoy Grieves for a Son / 14
Sonya Tolstoy's New Hat / 15
Death of Leo Tolstoy / 16
Photographing Dostoevsky 1 / 18
Photographing Dostoevsky 2 / 19
A Bolshevik's Father / 20
The Faith of a Bolshevik / 21
Witness to the Meeting Between Simone Weil
and Leon Trotsky / 25
Connemara / 27
Dorothy Wordsworth / 28
Poet's Travels / 30
Paradoxes / 31
John Berryman on Patmos / 32
On the Alleged Deathbed Conversion
of Wallace Stevens / 37
Flood / 39
Concubine / 40
Lapland Journey / 41
Before Winter / 42
Cherry Blossom / 44
Advice to Michael Faraday in Pursuit of a Wife / 45
Sarah Faraday's Dilemma / 46
Seminarians, Finckenwalde / 47

TWO
Emotional Map of Greater Belfast

Our Side / 51
Going Home / 53
Up from the City / 54
Castlecaulfield / 55
Turn-Coat / 56
Weak Point / 57
Slippers / 58
Travelling / 59
Emotional Map of Greater Belfast / 61
Baton / 65
Birthings / 67
First Marriage, Aged Fifty / 70
Mother to the Bride / 71
Visit to the New Hairdresser / 72
For Sale / 73
Reading Matters / 74
To a Poetry Friend / 76
P.T.S.D. / 77
Choosing Lottery Numbers / 79
Bed and Breakfast / 81

ONE

Tolstoy in Love

Anna Akhmatova

Let the moon take its bow in the serrated clouds.
Let the sun rise tomorrow with its orange-yellow
mouth aghast at the release of my son. Let his
cold hands and ravaged boots feel the warmth
of the melting Siberian snow. Let this applause rise
amongst these state-worshipping rafters,
their façade of gold stucco Gods. Let Stalin
in his high office listen to the whisperers
and let him feel this applause echo
through his ribcage. And let him know, and the agents
who will bug my quarters on Fountain Street know,
that the silver willow of my childhood
will rise again from the source of the earth
and soak up these waters of applause. And on
a God-given day, the wind light across the Urals
to Tashkent, it will keen no more, nor be imprisoned,
but will applaud with its own leaf gusto and send out
spores that will raise from my loved mother earth
the writers with freedom to express her lushness,
or that colourless season, without the fear of the silent,
silent men, with the *burr* of their stultifying buzz-saws,
hacking at your living, breathing, life-enhancing branches.

Tolstoy In Love

An oak's umbilical cords snare my boot,
snake the undergrowth through decomposing leaves
and lichen. Under the weeping canopy, my greatcoat
(trailing thirty-four years of memories)
drags me back to my first birth cries at *Polyana*.
Ahead, at the edge of Zaseka Forest,
sunlight slides through the thinned umbrella,
plays ribbons on the bare shoulder of Sofya Andreyevna.
She wears a white dress with the simplicity and purity
of the youthful stream that washes over her feet.
Palivanov approaches, in cadet uniform,
his military buttons glistening with stalks of light.
He sweeps you into a waltz, so light and fluid
you could dance on the backs of the swaying cornfields.
And I must watch, rest my head against
the oak's wrinkled brows, protest I am too old to dance.
In a murky pool I reflect my silhouette, my ugliness.
I am that Prince Dublitzsky of your novel.

Yet, an angel at my shoulder battles with my demons
pushes me forward into the sunlight. "Sonya!"
Light as wafted seed from a dandelion clock
she flies to me. I hold her hands. Her body,
aromatic, decants pomander and cinnamon.
She trembles like a wounded bird, blushes as if rouge
were applied to her cheeks. Is it too much to hope
to be made beautiful by a young woman's love?

Sonya Tolstoy

Above the yellow candle flame I watched
the corner pages of my script retreat in brown
and black waves, until I could hold the sheets
no longer. I tossed them in the fireplace,
mesmerised in the pallor of rising smoke ...

*In the cool of the evening kitchen garden
of Yasnaya Polyana, Lev Nikolaevich
lets me pick the ripening strawberries;
red juices stain my lips and fingers.
His workman's hand brushes against my dress.
A tortoiseshell, restless, flutters above
a pungent sea of mint and thyme.
I touch a brass button on his soldier's great-
coat, feel the contradictory warmth
and steel of his grey eyes assault me.*

*And I am off down the slope of a haystack
into the writer's safe hands. I am giggling
as he whirls me through the air;
in love with his deep, vibrant voice.*

*On the edge of abundant cornfields,
hair strains into the wind; my mare, Belogubka,
gallops in unison with the count's white horse.
As we enter the twilight of Zaseka Forest
hooves snap birch twigs and I hear
my mother call, "Sonya, come in for shelter,
come in for your bedtime."*

I stake a poker through the burning heart
of charred paper; the edge's silk petals
puff; gyrate in clouds of particles. Why,
why, did I show my beloved soldier-writer
this novice novel? In the hope his love was deepening
like the slow drip of water
collecting in the rain barrel at Polyana?

Love is a garden of palliative and bitter herbs.

The Jealousy of Sonya Tolstoy

Coming down this morning I found the door
wide open. A rank smell of dirty water
and rush of cold air intermingled at our threshold.
That woman, as if stooped in prayer,
worked, slowly, clockwise, with her wheezing brush.
We stopped. Recognized wife and mistress.
She folded back on sturdy haunches, withdrew,
holding me within sight of her defiant eyes …

In a desolate shed her ghost seeps under
my skin. I am chilled by the thought of seeing
her once more; of looking, again, into
the grey eyes of my husband's bastard son.
A page of his diary opens: 'Never so much
in love … *Peasants bend, plait sheaves
of hay. The sun concentrates on a bed
of hazel and maple. Lev tears at the blouse
like a pig snouting for truffles, unshackles
the breasts of his malleable serf …*
                              "Sonya!"
Outside, Aunt Toinette's feet scythe
tall grasses. I will leave this lair
at sunset. I will sit across the table from Lev.
The samovar will hiss and bubble between us.

Sonya Tolstoy Grieves for a Son

Maybe the formulaic babble of the priest
summoned me here. Or, perhaps, the stain glass
window refracting light from the emaciated
face of the agonised One.
                                        And yet, I ache
prayer, visit dank stations of confession,
imbibe thin wafer's dissolve, unreel
the creed, without solace, consolation …

In flight I clutch Alyosha's wings,
glide over Nikolskoye Cemetery
exposed to the north wind's scalpel.
A solitary dog howls as I scratch
at the earth's door, closed on Vanichka …

I inhale a sedative draft of wax
and incense, sweet fragrance of flowers.
Candlelight washes across my son's face.
Warmth of his breath aches through prairies
of day and night vigils, towards cessation …

Rain falls from Moscow's dank clouds,
penetrates to the roots of my tightly bound hair.
Vanichka rises, cradles me in the down
of his angel wings, to a break in the skyline over Kiev.
Shafts of light resolve in a spectrum
of colour. The touch and weight of Taneyev's
massaging pianist's fingers banishes
the black dog wailing at a veiled moon.

Sonya Tolstoy's New Hat

I lift the lid, respectfully, as opening
a bible. Rustle of tissue paper. I unwrap
the bonnet, stroke the sateen finish and raise
it from its nest, as if cradling a warm egg.
Eased on like a crown, it snuggles around
my ears. The dazzling white feathers
strain backward, over an unyielding brim.

The sun washes the room with light,
spreads shadow fingers through my doorway
along the corridor to Lev's hushed study.
My sister, Tanya, and Lyubov ghost behind.
Excitedly, I loop the blue Persian bow.

His eyes are cold. Wrinkles concertina
his forehead. He lays a pen down on a page
expansive with flaws.
                                        What? ...
A monstrosity. Why can't she wear her fur cap?
Tanya and Lyubov draw in deep breaths.

Distant, the sun's eye is being eclipsed,
paths ice over. I go to my trousseau
and set aside a woollen hat, a husband's
past favourite. I challenge the fading light;
we foray out, my Parisian hat's
carnival hour, before returning to the country;
our snow-locked home.

Death of Leo Tolstoy

Into the shock of winter's cold, gently
Sonya rolls, breaking the surface cleanly
as a dropped coin seeks a resting-place.
And when they haul you back, hair undone,
you shake off the wet dog excess, sob.

From beneath your pillow you unfold his letter
that pushed you to that pond, "My departure
will grieve you." Almost the killing blow …
News from Astapova:
footprints in dazed snow, plane trees
offended by the whirr of cameras. A continent
of hungry wolves assemble, push on closer
to the stationmaster's door. Tolstoy flickers
by the yellow candle flames, in, out
of consciousness …

Sonya follows, shunted into a siding.
Your presence is hidden; even a whispering
of your name is thought enough to extinguish
his flame.
                You push aside the buzzing media,
breath condensing on a window pane,
as you strain to catch a glimpse of Lev Nikolaevich.
You are admitted only after the portent plucking
at his blanket; the slow slipping into unconsciousness.
Your hand settles gently on his chest and you kiss
his forehead. A wheeze, as he exhales a last breath.

In the two-week delirium he ghosts back,
always with the accusing finger. And even
as you kneel on burning ice before his grave,
daily, the wolves are pressing in
with bared teeth, and a daughter is dipping
in black poisonous inks.
                                         A drawing in
upon yourself, as if for hibernation. Insisting
on routine, a waiter decants, in honour
of his memory. Wears white cotton gloves.

Photographing Dostoevsky 1

Penetrating the fomenting clouds the sun
cast its warmth over Puskin's
unveiled statue. Fydor Mikhailovich
spellbound our assembled crowd with measured words.
His sonorous voice was steady as the breeze
that fluttered the multitude of imperial flags.
And when he paused, our men abandoned hats
to the undercurrents, cheered each phrase idolising
our nation, our poet's genius. I knew then
that I must capture the essence of Dostoevsky.

Next morning I was pleased to see his eyes
were still on fire, as if hot ingots were plunged
into the Siberian snows of his sockets,
and cooled to the steel of his stern, determined stare.
First, we talked about that speech. He claimed
that as he spoke he felt Puskin's spirit close;
that the writers present spread before him,
through prairies, ice floes, forests, dispensing
Russian spirit beyond our nation's boundaries.

Behind the tripod I'd catch the visionary's
intensity of eyebrow, arched like the Urals.

Photographing Dostoevsky 2

Anna Grigoryevna allows tears to disperse
along the runnel of a dark-ringed eye;
presses her cheek against her husband's
sanitised face. She recomposes her mask
for friend and stranger, who spar in the drawing
room, waiting to touch the great writer.

Alone, in the minutes permitted, I assemble
the apparatus, breathe in the pungency
of censers, tears of tallow from tapered candles.
I angle across the glazed landscape
of the wax face, its hint of a smile;
at peace, at last, counsel to revealed truths.

Anna opens the door. The flood spreads
through the estuary. Slowly, lugubrious
faces, panoply of black suits stutter
around the dead novelist. I see Strakov,
Gradvosky, among the literati, who come
to pay tribute. Too late. They hide the knives
that ripped his Puskin speech
after their rapturous applause—and then what followed:
two epileptic seizures, extinguishing
a prophetic light, all over Russia.

A Bolshevik's Father

Harebells lean backwards as Father's boots whish past,
imprint gooey loam, squelch up a greasy embankment.
From behind a clump of dog-roses a hare bolts,
bobs into the sights of Father's rifle. Two pellets
puncture its back and hindquarters. A leg twitches
as he delivers the finishing shot to the cranium.

A skylark skims the pine-tops; its piping mingles
with the wind's hiss. In readiness, my father
sets his cocked rifle against the cart's side,
flicks open his army knife, incises the hare
and disembowels the slack creature. Its entrails
splatter his hands, jacket, warm June earth.

A friend throws word-bombs at Stalin:
laughter whooshes up like the jittery swallows
on a fence. The cart-horse shimmies, trots,
dislodges the rifle; lead scalds my father's chest.
Inside the womb I startle at the fatal reports.
For sixty years my hands will claw, resurrect.

The Faith of a Bolshevik

1

Sanya watched his mother, morning and evening,
drawn to the constancy of the votive candle's flame,
warmth of its closed tulip, glowing yellow to blue, down to the
    black wick.
She knelt beneath the icon; sing-song prayers burned into his
    memory.

2

Bolshevik horses' chattering hooves halted at the church door.
Out of brash morning light, high boots strode,
snow runnels loosed from their skin as they lumbered down the
    aisles,
rifles aimed at the few, mostly old, worshippers.

Sanya's mother lifted the two-year-old up through the fug
of incense and candle wax, to watch the soldiers blunder
against the Communion table; spilt wine staining the white cloth.
The aligned, flickering candles before the altar were extinguished.

3

Mother and son moved to a shack near Rostov-on-Don
where rain plopped in jam jars and tin trays arranged
on a stone-cold floor, beneath a corrugated tin roof.
A sough wind sang through gaps in the wooden wall-slats.

Indoors, winter was Siberian. And yet, Sanya's mother kept
a candle burning beneath the icon of gold-armoured Mikhail.
And when Grandmother Yevdokia died, his mother—her job
at risk—organized a mass in her memory at Rostov Cathedral.

Sanya fidgeted in the sepulchre-cold that day, counted
six others who might have felt the icy breath of the authorities
around their necks. Afterwards, he was summoned
to a draughty corridor outside the Headmaster's Office.

On a wall, above a stout desk, a framed poster of Lenin
composed its subject as if his eyes gazed beyond the Caucasus,
beyond the Volga to comrades transforming farm to collective.
Looking down, Sanya met the headmaster's dilated eyes

and mouth that shooed him away from the desk,
lambasted the boy, who flitted in
and out of the word-lashings; thoughts opening at
a picture of himself pinioned against a schoolyard wall

behaviour unbefitting a Pioneer   a hand reaching
beneath the ripped buttons of his shirt   *religious
superstition*   the cross torn from his neck   *faithful
to the Party*   thrown to corrode in a thorn hedge.

4

In the afternoon warmth of summer a crowd jostled on a Rostov
         street
to welcome back their exiled writer. A woman, haggard, stooped,
waving a photograph, pushed her way through to Solzhenitsyn,
"Remember this?" Sanya recognized himself; back row, third from
         left,

clean shaven, white collar overhang like a dove's outstretched wings
and, prominently pinned on his lapel, the Komsomol badge and
    insignia.
The face of Tanya, his fellow student, was composed as a calm lake.
Only later would she reveal that beneath the surface lay depths

of fear and pain: a father and uncle incarcerated, tortured in
    labour camps.
Sanya confessed to being oblivious of the suffering and plague
that surrounded him: *the swinishness of egotistical youth,* focussed on
hard work and fun, the university library, exams, theatre, concerts.

And as he spoke to Tanya, Solzhenitsyn felt, again, ropes of pressure
sear into his flesh, applied by schoolteachers and Komsomol leaders;
remembered how he grew to revere Lenin, his fist flung up, out-
    thrust jaw.
What a man! I believe to the marrow of my bones. I harbour no doubts.

5

Dragged through sludge and stench of a clay-pit, Solzhenitsyn's
    boots
weighed heavy as hardened cement. First ache of hard labour, the
    mud
adhered like glue to his shovel. He and partner Boris Gammorov
discussed Solovyev, poet—philosopher—Christian mystic

to keep their spirits up, but drudgery silenced their tongues.
Gammorov, exhausted, contracted tuberculosis.
His lungs weakened already by shrapnel, he died.
Solzhenitsyn cried; questioned his own *shallow atheism.*

6

Sanya, human cargo, was parcelled up again, transported by train.
Beyond the window the wind frisked mile after mile of meadows
and new-mown hay. He breathed in their scents; reinvigorating
    his senses,
a spiritual awakening before the door shut on Special Prison No. 16.

Here he was, a fulcrum in a triumvirate of seekers after truth:
Lev Kopelev, one end of a see-saw, clung to his Party card,
and yet, recipient of food parcels, he took a loaf, broke it in half
and gave to Panin, at the opposite end, who thanked God

for this man's nobility of spirit; for bread that tasted like manna. So,
three men satisfied their hunger for debate, never spilling into
    argument.
Sanya, uncommitted, rode see-saw vacillations, concluded,
I am deeply convinced that God participates in everyday life.

7

Post-operative, prison orderlies abandoned Sanya's bed in a recovery
    room,
a cold, ghost-like mausoleum. He was rigid as the bed's steel frame,
yet conscious for three fevered days and nights, when he would take
those final steps of faith to God, as he looked into the unmasked

face of death, and knew he might fall more easily into oblivion
than live. *God has saved me for a purpose.* When freed
he'd release two legions of lines, entrenched in memory,
and always, on his writing desk, a lighted candle weeping.

Witness to the Meeting Between Simone Weil and Leon Trotsky

1

Our dress and disposition to pass as bourgeoisie,
Trotsky's upturned collar itched his shaven face.
Strange to see him without his hallmark goatee,
his hands delving into greatcoat pockets.
Under the amber lights our breaths streamed,
interlocked with cold mist falling on beads of light
that glistened, settled on the Seine.

2

Pipe and cigarette smoke idled, fogged
the room next door to where Mademoiselle Weil,
by request, wrestled, alone with Trotsky.
I snuggled my hand around the revolver
in its greased holster, sat close to the door,
eyeing my three comrades, inert, alert for action ...
bull roars punctuated the stillness, the mock-
gothic table rattled with the steel of his emphatic fist.

3

I dallied while Trotsky and entourage hurriedly departed.
Mademoiselle portrayed an unruffled surface
yet I knew there were depths of will she'd plunged:
an arm branded with hot factory ingots;
a back stooped from gathering ripe corn in farm fields
aching with ravenous sun.

                               I was amazed
at how she'd held her own with Trotsky—
Counter-revolutionary, petite bourgeois.
He regurgitated his familiar high priest's litany.
We could have used her intellect, her vision. But here
I witnessed a young emaciated woman in dark
and ruffled dress, the repose and quiet of a nun,
not a revolutionary.

                              4

*Mademoiselle leans over my drugged
and dying body like one of her sham apparitions.
Surrounded by an aura her breath is shallow
on the back of my hand ... she hovers over the exiled
Trotsky, shaded in the cool of a concrete and glass
apartment, ink drying on a final mocking
draft. A report bloodies the ragged hair-
line of the Sierra Madre ...*
                                *I witness her now
in the barren fields of Ukraine, a wing-beat
above an open trench; stench of pale
and naked corpses. Upon peasant workers
she lets fall droplets of sweat from her
pain-wracked forehead, washes their feet
with her loosed hair ... ah, this vision trading
only on opiates ... poor deluded Mademoiselle.*

Connemara

Posthumous letter from Sylvia Plath to Richard Murphy

Dear Richard,

Forgive me for dying.
My mother put it kindly, 'some darker day',
impossible dreaming:
couple of *New Yorker* stories in Ireland,
dear dear wild Connemara
enough to drive a poet to madness,
Ballinasloe, Cleggan, Coole, Ballylee …
sailing the *Ave Marie* to Inishbofin.
And dear Tom. Did the strain show? I mean Ted
and I.
Sweet relief, warmth of milk straight from the cow,
the savoury smell of a real turf fire.
Remember how you helped me rent a cottage
next door to that sturdy woman—
I could have drawn on her strength, her language.

I still walk your shores; sea and horizon mingle
throwing up ghosts to meet an azure sky,
and little hummocks of rock, shining black seals.
My freakish head may appear again in the Atlantic;
sea-splash, and I wear a white gown of beautiful Nauset.
Then a malevolent swastika black sea clings,
and I must ride those horses back across London.
I would starve here intellectually
but for the muse of Yeats that blesses me,
your seas of isolation that sting as well as heal.

Dorothy Wordsworth

By your bed I find an apple-core;
its juices damp between my fingers.
I stroke its underbelly, fresh-water fish,
black entrails seeped towards the tail.
The serrated fins are like locks of seaweed;
the pips like brown, luminescent eyes.
I hold it to my cheek. Keepsake,
reminder of you.
                               I stub my toe
on your moss- and lichen-stained boots.
I'll scour the pebble punctured soles,
revive the black leather; the shine
rising like morning sun's water-mark
against Dove Cottage.

I kneel, gather William's pantaloons
and brown tunic from the floor;
press the bundle to my breast
as if comforting a child. Poor soul,
distracted by the cuckoo poem
he left in haste, early this morning,
leaving crumbs from only one lightly buttered,
decrusted slice.

I pick some snowdrops, arrange them
in the swan-neck vase, and place them
on the fresh linen table-cloth,
prepare the evening meal. Wait.
The apple core is safe beneath my pillow,
gently wrapped in a handkerchief.
Dearest brother …

                    At last
the fretting dog nuzzles the door;
your boot scrunch familiar as when
you pace the clinker track, turning
on the iamb, masculine endings.

I cross-stitch, long slow strokes
to form the lacy patterns
on a muslin dress, as William worries
a verse to completion …

We lie upon earth's snug glove,
the wind so deft that ash and alder
barely stir. John's Grove is splashed
with birdsong; our breathing shallow,
eyes closed   together.

Poet's Travels

Indeed, Boston, Washington, Philadelphia
were furthest, bodily, she travelled. Reluctantly,
one might add, for foreign scents of maple bloom

only made her yearn for familiar larkspur,
thrilling linnet, a homestead. Even to touch
on the memory of George Washington's latch

and glide down Potamac, bowed willow greening,
could not surpass the clasp of Lavinia's sisterly hand.
She scratched beneath the city's glitter, uncovered tarnish.

Home, a zephyr tumbled from the Evergreens;
Titicaca of unfathomable depths, prairie of knowledge
carried by the wind as song of nightingale,

until sister-in-law avalanched a Himalayas;
iceberg between familial houses. Barricaded
within a room and garden for fifteen years

she tamed wild orchids, macheted an Orinoco Basin,
intrepid as those botanists who bloomed from pages
of 'Flora and Fauna of the South Americas.'

Even the snow's death-mask on her garden
could not rebuff the robin's unique hieroglyphs.
And then the resurrection months when humble

buttercup splashed full and diminished suns,
when daisies closed their eyes
and shooting stars barraged an inner room.

Paradoxes

Caged in a doorway between garden and conservatory
the Peachfaced Love Bird trills a Niagara.
The family replenish seed and water.

Emily dead-heads red anemones,
allows sun to quiver along the backs
of her slender hands; listens intently

to the Song Thrush's warble. In an eye-blink
it's gone, rudder guiding through blue sky
to land on a school's nervy weathervane.

A tortoiseshell, tissue from bone of the sun,
alights on Emily's crinoline, as if stitched, integral
to the dress. Without warning, it's swallowed by hibiscus.

Her bedroom is spare as a Puritan pew.
Before writing she feels the cold breath
of her grandfather over her shoulder,

muddied spade in hand. She shrugs
him off, goes on tilling white acres;
pen-furrows natural as the bird's throaty song.

John Berryman on Patmos

1

An easterly breeze decants
from off the Aegean's blue
unruffled counterpane.

In mist the sun's asleep
behind the frayed edges
of Mt. Athos. Bell-toll;

otherwise unperturbed
the donkey cocks an ear,
clacks cobblestones

oblivious of weight
scissored against its back:
a man who hacks, licks

his lips, withdraws the tongue
into his mouth that's soured
this morning by strong brandy.

2

Tail swishes a horsefly and flanks glance
against an itch of jagged outcrop; hooves
traverse a lake of brush and baked earth.

In shade of tamarisk trees the hem
of a black Puritan dress touches
earth.   Anne Bradstreet?   *Mr. Berryman;*

*your face looks wan and drawn. Already, I feel
it is too late to withdraw from the rigours
of this journey. After visiting our house, partaking*

*of our hospitality—God knows we barely
had enough for sustentation of eight children—
you left, returned to a foreign century,*

*and I was glad; glad to have your warm breath
no longer bearing down on my starched collar.
But, Anne, we were one.   No sir, no,*

*I cannot even utter the words you used
to try and seduce me. Such sinful words
are as hot coals pressed upon my lips.*

*Yet sir, I come this morning, not to judge—
'tis true I struggled nights, alone, against
the sinful waves that crashed against my bed—*

but to urge, if you must *continue
this arduous journey, by the winding
stone-strewn track, do so at even pace—*

*do well to remember the burden of carrying
me, exclusively, for months: the exhaustion
of setting me down; slumping to bed for days—*

*sip often from Hora's spring,
but foremost keep your eyes fixed on the pinnacle:
monastery of St. John the Divine.*

3

For some minutes he rests at the side of the path and dismounts
and begins to unfold the stained hankie he's stuffed in his pocket,
then wipes the black rim of his glasses and swabs his lined forehead.
From behind there's a honk, a yellow taxi comes speeding on
    past,
its back blazing with sunlight, all windows wide open. And
    Berryman
is perturbed to see Frost on his own in a seat at the front.
At his shoulder, just behind, and squabbling and jostling are
    Lowell,
young Jarrell and Schwartz. So, the poet is mounting again;
bear-bellied, in the wind, his wild beard buffeted,
he's more grimly determined to make it to the top.

4

The sun, ungloved, hangs a necklace of heat
around the poet's bared throat and neck.
Each breath searches deeper into the lungs;
he gulps often from the lukewarm bottle,
readjusts sticky fingers around the reins.
Curled smoke drifts past his cheek,
and a father's ghost shadow at his shoulder.

When I gently closed the door of our apartment
early that cool June morning, stepped out
into the yard and pressed the .32 against my chest
I thought I'd put my damned world to rest,
eased into a hushed grave at Holdenville;
the wind through cottonwoods my sole companion.

*And yet I cannot rest, wearied by
the black cloak of grief in which I've clothed you.*

*Look across the bay: that speck on white sand
is your mother, yelling, hands flailing towards
a hump-back abutment. I bob above the waves,
your brother strapped to my chest. I'm dizzy,
far from shore. Your stepfather thrashes, plucks
at my back. And this is the cast I've bequeathed:
out of control, truculent, guilty, defeated.*

Father, don't. No need to beat yourself up;
after the Crash there was barely a block
where death's cut-throat hadn't visited.
I blame mother for taking *Uncle Jack* as a lover,
stoking too many coals into the raging fire
of your emotions. I've taken steel
from your ruin. Rest, now. I will press on.

5

Around the final corner,
rising from an icing
of flat-roofed dwellings
into a sea of blue sky,
the monastery, with towers
and turrets, resembles
a stout fortress or castle.

A lizard scampers over
the wall on which the poet rests,
dissolves down a trail
from where a woman appears

in ankle-length dress
and feathered hat, beneath
a laced parasol: his mother.

*How often must I try to knock away
the pedestal on which you deify your father?
His family snubbed me; set the tone for a cold,
inhospitable marriage. He was a weak man,
lacking in sexual vitality. God, Berryman
was like a winter storm that whips across
the beach and marram grass at Clearwater:
fresh, invigorating, potentially catastrophic.
Pity your father's business collapsed
when it did; love is no respecter
of good timing. I did my best for him:
removed the bullets from his gun, organized
for psychiatric help, all to no avail.
So, don't wag an accusing finger at me,
you can't resurrect the dead through your pen;
Why don't you sing my praises more?
Do you hear me? Do you hear me?*

"I faint. Quells her constant tongue.
Each telling she wears a new angle.
I see my father's dissolving footprints
all along Tampa Bay;
water weight breaks around his feet.

The gun, dull in hand. One bullet, left
sleeping in the barrel, bursts thru the chest
of morning blue. Lovers turn, hug,
snug. I find him slumped against steps;
boyhood shot. Betrayal of your name:
John Alleyn Smith."

On the Alleged Deathbed Conversion of Wallace Stevens

By spouting Longfellow perhaps you hoped
that naïve nurses would imbibe this sop,
deluded that the words were penned by poet-

patient who, while dangling from a rope
over a cancerous precipice, could joke,
engage in bonhomie. Maybe a way to cope

with dying. Or, perhaps, you'd come
to realize the imminent fall to the gorge
below, wagered a leap the only course.

Father Hanley claimed that you were weak, not doped,
that you reminisced on how you'd stolen from cold
cut-throat streets to sit at peace, composed

in St. Patrick's incense-swathed rows.
Three times requesting entry to the fold
a silver St. Christopher medal was bound

one side of your pillow, cross and chain wound
around the other. Sister Philomena eased the cope
over the top of vestments, passed a jot

of salt that stung the penitent's tongue.
Oils of catechumens and chrism were poured
on the crown of the head, *baptized absolutely.*

Yet, over the grave of Jesus, constantly
your breath was iced. So, to your daughter Holly
you told of how through your domain,

by dark of night, the priest had slithered, worried
you, and you almost too weak to complain.
Maybe both accounts were fact; comedic

ploy to play two cards from a pack that offered
many routes to heaven. And when you dropped
of course there was no splash, no sound returned.

Flood

At first it appeared as water-marks on our window
that we might wipe clean the stains.
Then more persistent, our feet sodden

we could no longer ignore the rising waters.
We barricaded the door with weighted sandbags,
crossed our fingers and kissed the hidden icons

and dared to lift our eyes to hill and sky
in search of refracted light's safe omen.
A raven kept encircling our house.

We returned to the comfort of armchairs,
the water slowly filling our aquarium.
Baby, secure in an upstairs bedroom,

was the last to drift away in sleep.
Immersed, the waters washed our bodies;
an olive leaf floating over our heads.

Concubine

Evening in the north the wind veers,
touches my cheek with its coolness:
The emperor is on leave from business.
The stone Buddha sprinkles waters
from the well of a dark and ancient throat
and water-lilies fill my eye.
I could throw my satins to the wind,
feel flesh burn in the fire of a God's cold eye.

I shall not enter the pomander and lavender room
to spread myself between earth and flesh.
I will lie with wind and water,
my breasts flattening to warm the earth.
They will find me with silks undone
and know that lust has gone to earth.

Lapland Journey

South, we followed the frozen Kemijoki
until Little Bread Eater collapsed
into the white ocean of fatigue,
as the fluffy waves turned blinding blizzard,
whipped up a majestic cathedral of white;
white heat that burned the eyes
and sent us to dive beneath the sleigh's cover.

We emerged tired, dog-tired; listened
to the crackle of the birch twig fire and tinkle of bells.
Bread Eater sank to a grey moss bed.
Nature *beseelt,* as I sipped camomile tea;
the hallucinatory cries of dwarf firs
in crescendo, singing in tongues to a sky
flecked by angels. Ground swell of goblins,
blue-capped, scarlet-ribboned, belts studded
silver lighting the forest. Carnival
of fairies, bright princes, aurora borealis ...

Cold stirs; necessity drives us onwards
to another world, transitory, a daydream
through poverty, a little sadness, fatigue.

Before Winter

Candles burn
    gentle yellow
flames around
    my grave.
Yet, you cannot
    hear my del-
icious laughter.
    Thirty-four
dying of cancer
    the jokes
grew blacker
    to the last;
for I could
    not die
any differently;
    could not
clutch at super-
    natural straws.
The only God
    I knew was
my makeup artist.
    His foundations
changed my life.
    Yet, I had
my commitments:
    the stripes
across my back,
    holding
the picket line.
    Just causes.

Let me feel
   the warmth
of my husband's
   resuscitating
lips; our child
   at my cold
breast. When he
   is older, tell
him, tell
   him how it is
here, ever-
   lasting disquiet,
without light
   without rest
without God.

Cherry Blossom

The flowers are hand-painted Belleek, parian cups
spilling yellow-honeyed seeds of flaked manna.
I stand beneath the canopy's umbrella, brilliant
as white-washed cottages that furrow distant
illuminated hills across the oils of Belfast Lough.
The shawl, embroidered white and greens, holds me.
Once I would have struggled to break free,
fallen from grace into a dandelion and burdock soup,
where stinging nettles confer with wild-eyed clover.
I lean against your signatures of muscle, dark-sinewed arms;
swim within your sinuous strands of fire-white beard,
and like the orange-beaked songbirds that blossom
on your wings, I will sing, sing, sing.

Advice to Michael Faraday, in Pursuit of a Wife

Hire a carriage and driver. Ride on the outside, at speed
through Kent countryside, huddled together against bracing winds,
she in Parisian bonnet and high Empire-line dress,
hair loosened, black streamer. Stop on the lee of Shakespeare's
    Cliff,
let her feel the rush of on-shore wind around her ashen face.
Remember, that day, submerge the scientist in you,
so when gulls hang on currents of air and do not flap their wings
for twenty minutes, do not analyse, take notes; but let a magician's
    fire
spark at the ends of your fingers; go blind towards the precipice,
inflame the waters below to sparkle, break in white waves, buffet
packet, sail ship. Here you might embrace the spontaneity
of nature's brushstroke: fleeting effects of light, shot reds
and yellow sky. And as a mist-veil lifts across Drop
and Redoubt, witness, distant, the conflict of dissonant sea currents
that meet in sudden upsurges, like fountains from a blow-hole;
look for changes in cadence of the sea, plash and turbulence
as it brushes sand and shingle, meets resistance of white cliffs,
and then winds might spear through the interstices of her heart.

Sarah Faraday's Dilemma

3 a.m., a candle flickers beside our bed.
Michael is fitful. Dearest husband, never
have I endured such pain. Up and down I tread,
nightly, uneven floors; pray to be delivered
from this agonizing: I contemplate with dismay
the loss of our Sandemanian birthright.
I cosseted you through marriage's dark valleys:
the breakdown; childlessness to my sisters' surfeit.
And if we are left to wither, out in the cold
will I have to choose between loyalty to church
or beloved husband? I am snug in the fold;
blindfold, perhaps, lacking my husband's searching
nature. But, questioning scripture? My heart groans
at your need, always, for testing. Faith, faith alone.

Seminarians, Finckenwalde

Supper. The brothers would not have heard
the shrill squeal of the knifed pig; witnessed
the squirt of warm blood on the butcher's boots;
animal collapse as swift as an executioner's
bullet to brain, heart.   On a brother's plate
both ends of bacon curl; the cured meat
crackles as knife and fork dissect; salty
aftertaste slaked with red wine;
adequate grape plucked from the lee
of Stettin's beechwood valley.   The brothers
have given thanks for local gifts; shanks of meat,
boxed fruit, aligned against cool storage walls.
Over plates' chatter, glasses' chimes
conversation flows   tightening rope
of Reich restrictions around the Church's
throat   Dietrich's interpretation of the Sermon
on the Mount: prayer   meditation   action …
                    The housekeeper requests,
"Will someone please help with the dishes?"
Five minutes, more, conversation continues.
Dietrich rises, quietly walks to the kitchen.
Some brothers follow; are gently turned away.
With dishcloth wipes, hands immersed in suds,
Dietrich works in silence.
                        Later he'd join
his brothers, sisters, in step beneath sycamores
that threw shadows over all of them.
He did not mention their inaction;
a gust across their sheepish faces
cut deep as any planted incendiary.

TWO

Emotional Map of Greater Belfast

Our Side

Crossing Main Street I passed by Grimes's
twin shops; the first with wine and pumice-
coloured flesh that hung from gooseneck hooks.
Shish of butchers' blades on a sharpening stone.
Sawdust curled in pigs' tails

on a blanched floor. The air ached cold,
yawning cold storage. Their brother confectioner's
had a spick glass-fronted window, scrubbed
deal counter and balance that gleamed like
a mint Queen's head on my sixpence or shilling.

And Bob, clean-cut, would hiss and wave,
always leaving me indecisive, halting,
slinking to McGurk's to surrender my trade
to *the other side:* the front room of a two-
up, two-down terrace with a partitioning

curtain, remnant flock, ruche-flowered,
from where crinkled Florry, in dark clothes
ghosted as if on wheels. Behind her
a whispering wireless was tuned to *Radio Éireann*.
That L-shaped, pokey sweet-shop was homely:

Love-hearts, liquorice and sherbet squabbled
across the scratched counter. With grudging light
straining through her windows, no superfluous
talk was traded, as she kept a suspicious
eye for sweets falling into wrong pockets.

Soon, I ducked and slunk past Grimes's
on our side, darted a diagonal between

Burrough's timber yard and Wells's General Store,
afraid of Bob's yells over my Protestant shoulder
like ice-wind from off the battlefields of Aughrim.

Going Home

On Sundays my cousin puts on slippers, between
church and dinner. Framed in a window, he's taken
up the stride of his father, grandfather, squelches
across the cobbled yard. Under the slate roof,
where once snug thatch slept, he rattles
the shut door. I shake his gnarled hand.
(Ten years ago we last met, exchanged, 'Sorry
for your trouble'). Allows no preliminaries
before he plunges into the dammed waters
of our beliefs, credos, "I suppose you were
at the *Twelfth* the year?" Clipped voices, smell
of boot polish, flash of orange regalia,
swirl of pipes, drums, distant as Aboriginal
sacred rites. Yet, close, momentarily,
to splinter the comforting *snip-snip* of secateurs,
hum of lawnmowers along a cultured cul-de-sac,
as *safe,* behind hedges I try to keep in check
rampant flames of ragwort.

And so, my cousin, you and I, earthed
in the same Tyrone roots, have grown
up acres, drumlins, neon lights apart.
As you lead me, my two sons, past John
Sloan's abandoned patch, I try to understand
your need for certainities: Carnteel Presbyterian,
Cabbragh Orange Hall.   My deckshoes wedged,
precariously, between two caked slices
of slurry, I measure the distance of your nearest
neighbour as beyond a yelp. A neutral lapwing breaks,
tremulous, below a threatening blue-black sky.
My cousin strides on, in firm, unbroken footprints.

Up from the City

Under a counterpane of billowy clouds
I rummage for rainwear, stouter shoes
to follow my cousins around the farm.
And they, sleeves rolled, in Sunday slippers.
First plop of rain they saunter into a shed.
"Only a wee skiff". Fists of rain thrum against
the flat roof, as a green *Massey* burgeons
from the floor. I barely lift the plough's sock,
"Heavy" … "Naw, not too bad …"

Rain eased, gingerly I follow the rutted
track, along the middle stream of untamed
grasses, while you step lightly, as if
traversing hot embers.
                        I shelter under
an umbrella of beech leaves, as sough wind,
arrows of rain pierce us. Fuss into my coat.
Cousin Tommy smirks, "Nae call for thon".
Beads of water bleed through his shirt.

They shunt open sliding doors, leap
puddles of bilge and dung, while I skirt
the edges, follow into a cold barn.
Along one wall the bales of hay lie haphazardly.
"Wanst this place wud be full if hay …
Down in Augher I'd giv Joe Clements
a haun til shift his feed. When I clim
among the bales the rats, as big as cats,
runs over me hauns, lashing out with their tails."
Tom holds my eye, follows it down from the stacks
to his dog slobbering at my hems. Hold my ground.

Castlecaulfield

I drive down a linear street pockmarked with memories,
last greeted twenty-five years ago, and wonder where
the people have gone on this dank Sunday afternoon:
Paul Laughran and the *tap tap* of his white stick;
Tom Weir in his front window, prinked and preened
by his wife, who bound his bales of hair with rollers;
John Nugent and his cranked A40 anchored
outside his front door, in hoary frost and sunlight;
sweet-talking Rosie, his mop and brush co-worker
at Parkanaur's Disability and Retraining Centre;
Aggie, John's roly-poly wife, behind the cabin door
kept the decks scoured, as greyhound faces
nosed blinds, sniffed over barricading drumlins,
high hawthorn bushes—at anyone, anything out of alignment.

Passing on, I point out to my two sons the cobbled lane
that leads to Clananese Glebe, where unwashed Sandy Bones
cultivated an acre beneath his fingernails;
the closed door on Main Street where I grew
tall as the bamboo that flourished beyond the river
on Truesdale's demesne, opening for a few seconds only
a child's view of Amazonian undergrowth
on the lip of the Blackwater, its trickle in summer
allowing the *whoo* and *whoa* crossings of stepping stones
to meet the bulk of Caulfield Castle's ruins and the black rag
rooks dropping to roost. I once leapt from those walls,
sank in tufts between thistles and unleavened cow pats.

Now, in contact with this street again, I'm like a son
drawn back to his mother, despite her many blemishes:
the fixity of street scents infects my imagination;
smoke billows from the frozen lips of the factory stack.

Turn-Coat

When I see greys I think of Charlie Woods,
a true trooper, swearing at his wife,
who being a fine church-mouse all her life
would laugh it off (*Glory be to goodness*)
in front of a line of white long-johns

worn by Charlie in the summer sunshine
as we sat like sentries at his front door—
white cuffs showing as he poked the foreground
with a blackthorn, and talked to a child
man-to-man without a hint of starched bravado:

teaching me how bees don't sting
if you hold your nerve and hold your breath.
Behind, the cats would pad past steamy broth
and Kerr's Pinks, to leap from table to settee
where I'd somersault for hours without a scolding.

Down South you rode in point-to-point
and afternoons we'd watch the racing on TV.
When picking winners from the pack, you'd reject
the grey in favour of a sleek and shining chestnut.
Sadie would always round us up for tea ...

I see greys and think of Charlie Woods
in turn-coat colours, flogging a dying horse,
six-foot frame too awkward for this course,
black horse straying North; a wife supportive
as he curses past family and church to the finishing line.

Weak Point

Too thrawn to attend doctors, you'd rather thole the pain;
a surgery only for the *weak, weemen* or *weans*.
Polytar Liquid Shampoo, emulsifying ointment
twinned in the bathroom—for weeping eczema you'd sent
mum to the chemists, afeard to be thought a Jinny.
Self-esteem was fatal. Half that night you futtered, gaunch-
like, until submitting to the South Tyrone, to staunch
a stubborn nosebleed. Soon I'd wake to that phone-call:
how you'd collapsed, suddenly, at Loughgall Football Club.
The haemorrhage would leave you to vegetate, if hauled
back; you'd approve as lights went out, beyond that hubbub,
not limping out, girning, crippled to the finish.

Slippers

Each morning he takes his slippers off; leaves them
beside his corner chair and laces up his boots.
He chivvies his sprawling daughters, who push past
in flexing trainers. Their father's footwear stamps
across the kitchen tiles that lead him through the threshold
into daylight and the fields.
                                      His wife, behind, in pumps,
clatters dishes, stirs her daughters to action,
who bend, tuck in untied laces, forage
for schoolbags, books, gym-shoes.

Their dad returns by lunch-time, as steam
rises from the kitchen hob. He unshackles
his sweating boots, scatters them and slips
the tartan slippers around his clammy feet.
Already the partitioning door is open;
his wife's made several crossings. He strides
across his wooden floor and tentatively
steps on the warm ceramic tiles, into the kitchen
he has crafted. Still, above his head,
he recollects the weight of thatch, the jug and basin
by his bed, the slap of water awakening him
and his bare feet on stone cold floors.

Travelling

1 ESKRA LOUGH

We took our ease that day,
so hot on Ballygawley Road
that tottie stones plumped,
stuck to our soles.

                  After a half-mile dirt
                  track to Eskra Lough's
                  dark basin, we sat
                  on an uncultivated hill

near tufted, yellowing grass,
whins and wind-tousled
broom's hair. My mother
and father lit cigarettes

                  wafted smoke at the cloud
                  of midges nipping
                  at our skin. The towels we spread
                  were skimpy as handkerchiefs.

We looked down at the cut
of a pair stripped off
to trunks and a bikini, brown
as berries and swaggering about

                  showing off their tans
                  from somewhere foreign,
                  from somewhere beyond
                  wrapped drumlin, wet Sperrins.

I tip-toed, as if the ground
would scorch my feet;
as if those thistles
were markers for a slalom,

                              down to Eskra's sour,
                              sullen lip. She lay
                              like a dormant animal
                              presenting a smooth skin
unruffled fur.
My uncle, who could
swim her mile stretch,
would tell how she shelved
                              away, quickened her depths
                              threw down shafts to an abyss,
                              clamped the unwary. For he,
                              on that hot afternoon tried
to prepare me for my journey:
his cupped hands beneath
my back and legs. *Relax.*
I stiffened, resisted,

                    spluttered air and water
                    from the mouth's blow-hole,
                    inhaled slime stagnancy, trying
                    to break away from constricting rushes.

Emotional Map of Greater Belfast

1. ARRIVAL

On this, his first visit, my artist cousin uncurls
a map of Greater Belfast, brings with him
a baggage of colours transported from Manhattan
to his studio in pollution-conscious Portland.
They'd smear blood-red across this city's
northern quarter, plumes of smoky black
igniting in nightfall messaged bottles,
flame-green flak jackets and scowl
of riot shields overlapping in pale washes.

2. THE FIRST TEMPTING

Looking down from Napoleon's Nose I tempt
you to paint a troubled scene. No need
to finger the terraced rows below,
we'll delve in archives at the Linen Hall
uncover skinny lads in scruffy clothes
posed before a smoking burnt-out van
with hands and scarves to mask their faces.
Perhaps you'd add a cudgel to the smallest nipper's hand
and paint the eyes less harshly; big and watery
and sad. Some sap green and ochre, soft blue
and yellow to smooth the hard edges of the canvas.

3. THE SECOND TEMPTING

Or might I tempt you tonight from the tallest
rooftop to look north: two bridges straddle
passive Lagan's mauve and blues. The quayside
lights submerge as apparitions, or tiptoe
as angels swayed by the genteel plash of water.
Distant, unpeopled, the city sparkles with clusters
of mellow suns and stars, and arcs of red
and yellow half-moons.
                                            Above,
the sky is stroked with salmon pink and muted
turquoise releases a genie of dispersing blue
into misty-eyed, chocolate-coated hills.

4. RESOLVE

I offer you these options, assured that either way
you'll make a killing, back in the U.S.A.
I make you think about the spin-offs: posters,
postcards, the tea towel images …
                                            But
looking down you won't be bound within
these hills and lough and sky. Your eye decodes,
your hand will sift the pieces of an elaborate

jigsaw, etch in black and white the keys
of distant terracing that slots in perpendiculars,
horizontals as if to form the façade of a Roman
temple. It bleeds its reds to the north of the slate-
grey, curvaceous Lagan.

5. THE JOURNEY

Stormont

We balloon down across the city.
I flick through a tourist guide, *What to See,*
veer towards Stormont's Portland stone
and hover over the hum of coaches. Its flock,
unleashed, are clicking Sam or Mary-Beth before
the mile long steep incline.
                                    Wanting more,
you throw out ballast. We rise above the uniform
rows of lime trees, dip for you to pluck
a bunch of broom, in open fields
beyond the Ice Bowl.

Tullycarnet

                       As we soar above
Langholm, Stornoway and Selkirk's high-rise
flats, you put the broom in an endangered
living window, with tieback curtains as parenthesis.

Annadale

Upwards
       and
               onwards we view the Lagan from Annadale.
At ground level, road and railings and river
are understated, bland. Only the people
looking downward, introspective, draw
on blue and brown and yellow, as perpendicular
trees and lighting pull the eye to the skyline.

The treetops are delicate as dandelion clocks; a breath
might feather their leaves to the distant liquid
horizon where sycamores red-tongue the sky.

Shaftsbury Square

You simplify the colours:
all lines swirl, flood
as black and red rockets.
White tail vapours
intersect in a splash
of orange; white
slicks, a fluid screen.

Diptych

It could be any back street
near the Hammer or Lower
Ormeau. A wall is daubed
with conflicting flags,
graffiti. In front you extract
the features of an old man;
glasses, not quite fitting,
corrosive teeth, face
etched with fault-lines,
wide, hospitable smile.
At his feet the pigeons pour
over pockmarks. Several
congeal in a many-
headed mass. One
with wings outstretched
rises into clear
tranquil blue.

A mother, exhausted,
lies full-length
on a bed of straw.
Her baby is pale, delicate.
The nurses in Mater & Ulster
uniforms crouch between
the snorting donkeys, look
at the mother's broad
smile. Two windows,
partially open, are rapped
by symmetrical branches
of a tree that rocks
backwards and forwards.

Baton

That morning he clasped me by my tapered end,
squeezed me in his hand until my black sheen warmed.
His polished boot stubbed the carpet and we tumbled
on the floor, spilling a bowl of white chrysanthemums,
as water and blood trailed from the broken jardiniere.
She came downstairs, running, as the letterbox
flapped open, snapped shut.
Letters cascaded, lay sullen, spread-eagled on the doormat.
He opened an eye, before she spoke, offered her hand.
He rose, slowly, like a felled oak; creaked,
swore, limped.
                    Unharmed, he wiped me clean
in an unfolded handkerchief; gently,
eased me into my snug leather bed.
We bruised past her cotton night-gown.

The fifth night we'd lined up like a squad
of blackbirds jittery on a wire. Closing the gaps
he beat me against his shield in rhythm
with his brothers. A bottle arced the night sky,
maddened the line with blue-yellow flame.
We made another rush. I pushed away a half-brick
into the petrol pungent air, injuring our arm;
a trickle of blood coagulated along my spine …

Off duty, he carried me in his car
twinned with his gun. The scent of an unfamiliar woman
mingled with the wind from off the lough.
He held her hand more tenderly
than ever he held me. Quick steps over
rough gravel. The passenger door was ripped

open and I saw a hand swing, slap
the face of the unfamiliar woman. *Bitch!*

We entered our home before the locks were changed.
The youngest son sat at the kitchen table,
remembering, perhaps, the past months:
a house embattled, his daddy drawing in
to his garrison, the setting off of distress signals.

Birthings

1

Beyond your window a rook rises
three stones' throw from Stormont;
lands on a solemn statue of Carson,
whose raised finger is directed down
an uneven pitch, adjudicating
all heretical incumbents *out*.
And yet the clans assemble, locked
in a ringed forum.

2

Your waters break; reflex leg
dunting your husband from settee to floor.
Your bulk slaps against the car seat;
engine whines past a Stormont side-gate.

3

At first the path is smooth.
Then negotiating a steep incline
a camera fixes on a pressured face
opening a window.
                         A northern rain
falls on the expectant pack
hounding the partitioning mesh.
Emissaries emerge—white breath
haloing from their mouths; prepare

us for a night vigil. We await
the coming forth, an unfurling of a new map,
assented, witnessed, signed.

4

In some distress. He waits before a fontanelle
in skull cap, sterile gloves, green gown.

>All rush, ushered
>through swing-
>doors, side-views
>his wife's brailled
>forehead. The doctor
>plays the forceps,
>rights the sideways
>child, sliding
>from the slipway—
>hauls him into air.
>The nurse hovers,
>wipes, coddles in cloths,
>presents to mother
>& father, smiling
>back at a black-
>hair mirror-image.

5

The senator reads the closing address
before the mannered smiles. A mile
away a wren taps its beak at a ward
window. The sleeping child rolls

from the mother's breast, as she looks
beyond the budding cherry,
unaware this birth is presage to
embryonic birth, light or dark …

Above the thrum of Lambeg and boreen
in unison, the rags of rooks sob
towards the hinterland, stained byways:
Darkley, Loughgall, Lisburn, Loughinisland.

Distant, the city, uneasy, buds with sun.

First Marriage, Aged Fifty

I turn my back, unshackle my breasts, untouched
by a male since I was nineteen ...
As my husband folds his trousers along the seams
the wardrobe's mothball whiff peppers my nose.
He lays his palm between my shoulder blades
like a soothing poultice. First sight of his bare feet;
stained with a brown wash, broken veins
stipple the ankles in purple outcrops. A window
is open to the warm night air ... *we carry our mattresses
and calico sheets onto the missionary roof.
In the distance Japur melts under the heat band.
Night sweats, dysentery, thoughts
of home; our cobble-stoned lane in back-
water Cabbragh; our first furniture: orange
boxes, a single bed shared with my sister
its sag and squeak familiar as poverty ...*
Cold, white bathroom tiles creak
beneath my feet. I shiver. In a knee-length
white transparent nightdress I kneel
beside the scrubbed white ceramic bath.
Fresh spearmint toothpaste tingles; slightly
numbs the mouth ... I pull back the duvet
enter the cool blue sheets; settle into the side,
cold this three years. You reach across the divide
link my hand with yours, gently.

Mother to the Bride

Those hands would knead a child's stooped head
as if applying carbolic along ribbed beads
of singing washboards, or stoking quagmires
of steaming clothes, doused in froth and suds,
while lip-reading through the steamie's fog
and chattering chorus.

Those hands would rise for you at 3 a.m., break
the ice, snap sticks, light the outhouse
boiler, stoke and pummel a mass of clothes
in a seething cauldron, peg and raise, criss-
cross a yard, enclosed, in shade. A wash
that flapped against the unction of dark clouds
slow moving over uniform tenements.

And now those hands, grown gnarled, arthritic,
have gauged her body lose a pound each week
since the engagement. And yet, determined,
fumbling, drawing blood, she tacks the hem,
stitches and smooths with steaming iron
her daughter's gown.

Today, those hands will hold the shaking stem
of a champagne glass, watch the fizzing liquid
froth and bubble over the lip, consent to toast
her daughter's happiness, in a room ablaze
with starched white tablecloths.

* *Steamie = Public washhouse*

Visit to the New Hairdresser

I slither into the chair, slouch. You flounce
the wrap and instruct me to sit up straight.

The undercurrent settles on my chest and torso
as you discipline the corners into my collar.

Cold spray squirts my head, stirs from torpor
like a slap across the knuckles. Your hands tousle

the hair into verbs and exclamation marks
before you propose the style of the composition.

You comb the strands of each sentence, abbreviate
with the *snip-snip* of scissors. Punctuate

new paragraphs through the scribble of pop
from the radio, as I submit to your guiding hands.

"Don't you remember me?" I cut to your double
in the mirror. Under a mask of peroxide

I recognise your flame hair. In parenthesis
I add, "Essays always daubed with red biro.

The chance to get your own back." Your face
is stern. Fingers correct the line of my neck.

For Sale

one used body, neatly presented by its present owner,
but requiring some internal renovation.
Only with a fuller inspection can one appreciate
the idiosyncratic style of this Comber dwelling.
Upstairs the garden is fenced for privacy
and overlooks open fields of the unconscious ...
Spotted brown cows dot a green baize,
brush uneasily against a surprise of red poppies.
Grazing cattle drink from the flooding Enler.
A tortoise shell, trapped in a spider's web,
displays a charcoal, brown and black underbelly.
Red-orange wings, rimmed with blue,
are splayed as if to fly ...
Downstairs, the heart of the house
is prone to sentimentality;
an early inspection is highly recommended.

Reading Matters

Cordelia clutches a copy of *One Hundred Years of Solitude*
by Gabriel Garcia Marquez, as she is transported on an
    undulating magic carpet
which exhales the whiff of jasmine, pomegranate and sandalwood.
She circumnavigates the room, hair a black streamer, taffeta dress
stitched with thousands of cold star sequins, and decanting an
    aromatic cocktail
of Dar Es Salem, Timbuktu and Rio de Janeiro.

She stops, sudden. Engages the hand of her former friend, Brenda,
who's posed in her graduation photograph of 1963. Brenda nibbles
on *salt and vinegar*, sips and postures over the rim of a Cognac
    glass
as they exchange reminiscences, the what-are-you-doing-now
    routine.
Cordelia tells of leaving teaching, ten years ago, to write.
Winters out on Achill Island, with the call of the curlew, slap
of Atlantic salt wind across marram grass to the white-washed
    cottage,
without electricity, running water, reading and writing by the light
    of a Tilley lamp.

Brenda boasts, "I haven't read a book. Not since 1963."
Perturbed, Cordelia flies, negotiates the traffic to the dining room.
Salome dances by with salmon displayed on a silver-plated platter,
spiced with paprika and oregano. To move clockwise or anti-
    clockwise?
Passes Pancho Villa with Paul Muldoon, still debating the subject
of the poet's craft, while Larkin smirks at the book cabinet,
its flock of mock Moroccan, barely fingered volumes
crushing paperbacks with tarty covers, cowgirls, lassoes,
    bucking broncos.

The sound of music wafts around the glutted table. Strauss or
 Mozart?
Cordelia daydreams … Officers gather for a private audience
with a mishmash Auschwitz orchestra which occasionally strikes
 a discordant note.
Nonetheless, notes of polite applause rise to the rafters. Abrupt
 endings.
A colonel retires, with a flickering candle flame, reciting from
'A Book of Hours' to dying strains of 'Eine Kleine Nacht Musik'.

Cordelia, in flight, leaps across Brenda's synapses, opens
 darkened
rooms and leaves the poem she's crafted. Knows the door will close.
Sometimes she wonders if she'd left the party early, would it matter?

To a Poetry Friend

For Iain

It is simpler if we undress her,
reduce the possibilities. For this
I stand on the shoreline, look
out of the wrong end of a telescope

across the oils of Belfast Lough …
Awaken you in a high-rise flat,
your pamphlet, lying on a well-made bed,
dedicated to the memory of a mother
and father for whom you sacrificed all trade.

Now you wear the shadow of long afternoons
between waking and friends. Your breath
passes from shore to shore over
the body of the woman we both
love   share   desire.

P.T.S.D.

dunnamanagh
                        wore
                                   a dreich day
as I trod
               with inchthick leather shoes
into
        omalleys bar and
                                off licence ...

quickening
               my pace
                          a white chevy
                                            convertible
red flash
              screaming down
                                side
                                        panels
corpses
            fornenst greenbaums
                                    minimart
and drugstore
                on west fiftysixth ...

gloss   of beer and blood
                               pouted
on floor ceramics
                    mirrored
a body   piked ...

```
behind
          a woman    birothin
blue rinse buffoned
                              in white
asshug shorts
              strains   to control
two panting   tonguelolling
                          dachshunds
              feline
                  i leap
hug
     her bones


DONTPASSTHATCARDONTPASSTHATCARDONT

                                    popeyed she
releases
          hold of
                   maniacal
                          yapping
                                 dogs ...



              the coroner's
                              soft hands
teased
       bullets from the kidneys
                                 clink
                                      clink
in the dish
            below
```

Choosing Lottery Numbers

Two. First on my card. The twins' yelps
first heard at two in the morning. Drew
sustenance from the Lagan and Tyne:
behind a riveter's shield, oxyacetylene
flamed the steel of two brute cities.

Fifteen. Age I left grammar. By Monday—
Is it on Monday that John comes to visit?—
I was shovelling hair, sharpening a cutthroat
on a leather strop, passing on the soft
bristled brush and mug of frothy water.

Twenty. Nightjars squabbled on telegraph wires
as the salmon pink sun melted
behind Table Mountain. Tyres squealed on
a cobbled alleyway and four M.P.'s launched
volleys. I froze. Yanks, trigger-happy.

Twenty-six. End-of-terrace tenement.
Pigeons fissled, rat-like, above our heads
as seagulls, dunted inland by hunger,
sniffed out crumbs from the bakery below
and I inhaled warm doughy smells at our window.

Thirty. Convoy of ships sailed from Durban
to Mombassa. At tiers of canvas-shaded stalls
woodcarvers squatted; wood chippings, squiggly
pigs' tails, languished at sandaled feet.
Stain glass rainbows were cut and shuffled.

Forty-nine. Years together. Inside
the house she had a magician's touch
conjuring ribbon after ribbon of work
until blades of pain cut and bled. Outside,
she was a mouse trapped at an electric fence.

Bonus? Fourteen. That day, in July—tubes,
wires invading the privacy of her flesh—
she began the slow process of dying.
I wanted to substitute myself. Couldn't.
Win? Luck's run out. Habitual card.

Bed and Breakfast

There is a sea of white tablecloth between
my wife and I and the couple breakfasting
at the end of the table. They have tacked beyond
orange juice, cornflakes, marmalade and toast
to mushrooms floated on a bed of cream sauce.

After teacups are stirred and teaspoons rested
awkwardly on saucers, we exchange the stilted
conversation of strangers. And yet, the woman
is open as the green fields that stretch beyond
the French windows to distant Mendips.

At home, in Cirencester, her mother has Alzheimer's,
is bedridden since the stroke two years ago …
Tom and Rosalind trudge up and down
stairs, night and day; her mother's cries
from a dimly lit room,

a mind that stumbles beyond closed blinds
leaps over cobblestones of childhood memories …
Rosalind's husband, Tom, goes on
lathering beans on the rump of a forked sausage,
"We escape when the opportunity arises," he says,

speaking only to his wife's eyes, which turn
in our direction, as if to deflect his words.
"Any plans for today?" I ask, and her eyes
bat back, "Hiring a couple of bicycles,
riding up to Glastonbury Tor."

After a long rest, having strained to the top,
they freewheel down, allowing a breeze to balloon
her loosened blouse, chalk-coloured face
pink-tinged, and Tom, in the slipstream of her laughter,
sailing after. Momentary spiralling to forgetfulness.

Printed in the United Kingdom by
Lightning Source UK Ltd., Milton Keynes
138576UK00001B/15/P